Stand Out!

How to Master
Your Next Job Interview

TONY CAPUTO

FREILING
PUBLISHING

Copyright © 2022 by Tony Caputo
First Paperback Edition

All rights reserved. No part of this publication may be reproduced, distributed, or transmitted in any form or by any means, including photocopying, recording, or other electronic or mechanical methods, without the prior written permission of the publisher, except in the case of brief quotations embodied in critical reviews and certain other noncommercial uses permitted by copyright law. For permission requests, write to the publisher, addressed "Attention: Permissions Coordinator,"
at the address below.

Some names, businesses, places, events, locales, incidents, and identifying details inside this book have been changed to protect the privacy of individuals.

Published by Freiling Publishing,
a division of Freiling Agency, LLC.

P.O. Box 1264
Warrenton, VA 20188

www.FreilingPublishing.com

PB ISBN: 978-1-956267-93-8
eBook ISBN: 978-1-956267-94-5

Printed in the United States of America

Dedicated to all of my mentors and my family for their support and encouragement.

Contents

Introduction vii
1   Replace Negative Emotions with Positive Actions 1
2   Gain Control of the Room 13
3   Setting the Stage 25
4   How to Ask the Right Questions 33
5   Align Strengths with Needs 43
6   The Likeability Factor 53
7   Tell Me About Yourself 63
8   Questions You Should Never Answer 75
9   Questions You Should Avoid Asking 85
10   How to Talk About Your Education 93
11   Getting Personal without Getting Personal 99
12   What About Your Attire? 107
13   Closing Strong 115
14   Mastering Video Interviews 123
15   The Post-Interview Follow-up 131
16   The Offer 139

Introduction

I'VE SPENT MY entire career in roles that require me to identify the best talent and maximize productivity and the results. If I learned anything along the way, it is that it is very difficult to determine those who will succeed and those who will struggle based on the initial interview.

Whether someone has a college degree or not, their mindset and ability to take action will likely be one of the most significant factors of their success. My goal in writing this book is to provide a practical set of steps that can help readers illuminate what's most important to the interviewer and secure that new opportunity that could change the course of their life!

DID YOU SPEND countless hours practicing *something* when you were a child? Maybe you played the piano, and your fingertips hit the same keys over and over until the piece was just perfect for the recital. Maybe you and a friend would shoot hoops for hours on end, playing H-O-R-S-E until you perfected your shots. Maybe you used flashcards to memorize words or mathematical equations. Of course you did. We all did these things. Practicing was, and is, an important part of growing up. We intuitively know this as adults and parents, and we encourage our children to practice. "Practice makes perfect," we tell our children.

Yet most of us fail to practice or prepare for one of the most important events in our lives—the job interview. Your role as a job applicant and the time you spend in job interviews undoubtedly has more influence on your income, your lifestyle, your well-being, and your future than anything else you'll ever do. It is the quintessential make-or-break experience. Other than choosing who to marry, there is probably no more important decision you'll ever make than choosing *how* to interview for a job. You will probably spend more time at work than you do at home with your spouse! Imagine if you dated like you did job interviews: hapless, unintentional, and accidental.

A great job interview absolutely changes the trajectory of your life and the life of everyone around you, particularly your family. Conversely, a bad job interview also changes your life but in a very different way. Yet, despite its importance, many people don't take time to prepare or practice for a job interview. Most don't even seek out that much advice.

Why don't we spend more time preparing for job interviews?

Interviewing for a job is certainly an irregular experience. Sometimes years may separate

Introduction

one job interview from another. Most of us will interview for a new job only a few dozen times in our lives, if even that many, hardly enough to spend much effort preparing for it. Also, job interviews often occur when we least expect them. Sometimes, we don't have much time to prepare, even if we wanted to. We literally don't think about it much until we walk into an office and sit down in front of the interviewer.

Jack had recently graduated from the University of Illinois with a master's and a Ph.D. in chemical engineering. After many years in the classroom, he was eager to get to work on his career, and he interviewed for a junior chemical engineering position at General Electric. The interview went well as Jack was ever-confident and displayed as much business savvy as he did engineering prowess. He was hired on the spot, and he worked his way through the ranks of one of the world's biggest companies. He eventually landed the job of CEO, the youngest to ever hold the position at General Electric. By the time he retired, Jack Welch was known as one of the most successful and influential business leaders in modern business history. He earned more than one billion dollars.

What if Jack's job interview at GE had gone poorly? What if he stumbled over his answers and blurted out something embarrassing or irrelevant? What if he dressed inappropriately for the occasion? What if all of his education went to waste simply because he walked in unprepared and just let the interview happen? Then we may have never heard of him. But Jack Welch was too smart for that, and he probably would have succeeded wherever else he went. But surely, his entire career at GE and as a business leader hinged on his very first job interview. You may never be Jack Welch, but I guarantee you won't even get the chance to grow in your career unless and until you begin to take your job interviews more seriously and approach them with a different mindset. Jack Welch didn't write about this first job interview nor discuss it with anyone,

Introduction

so we don't know what tactics he used. But it's fair to say he did his research, asked some key questions during the interview, aligned his skill sets with the most important aspects of the role, and also probably shared some of his plans to be successful in the job. Most importantly, I'd say he had a superior mindset going into the interview. These are the things I want to teach you. I want to teach you to STAND OUT!

I'm glad you're reading this book because it means you are looking for help. You're already at the top of the "pile" because most people don't look for help. Most people try to wing it. So congratulations! You might already be in the middle of the interview process; you might even have an interview tomorrow (or even today). Rest assured, I can help. I want to transform the way you interview for a job, just as I've done for so many others. There's no better feeling in the world when someone tells me, "Tony, we did it! I got the job!"

Everything you'll read in this book surrounds one basic premise: You can control the job interview in a way that makes you Stand Out from the rest. You don't have to let the job interview just happen to you, and you don't have to go into each job interview worried about how it will go. I'm going to show you how to go from interview victim to interview champion.

The following pages and chapters will show you *how* to take more control of your actions, be more confident, and go into each interview with a pre-established plan, a method that is proven to work. You'll be surprised at how easy it is once you adopt it and begin to use my strategies. It doesn't entail tons of research for each job interview. My method is a once-and-for-all solution that will work for each and every interview you'll ever do. This book is a methodology, a winning formula

> You can control the job interview in a way that makes you Stand Out from the rest.

Introduction

to help you STAND OUT at your next job interview. Follow the steps, and I guarantee you'll be more confident and prepared. When you walk into an interview, you'll be less anxious, more relaxed, more relatable, and more likeable. At a minimum, you'll greatly improve your odds of receiving a job offer

Why should you listen to me and follow my advice?

I'm a professional sales coach and experienced CEO, so I know a few things about sales and what type of employees companies are looking to hire. I've spent countless hours preparing for and successfully presenting products and services to clients, both small and large. This is how I worked my way up through the corporate ladder to serve as CEO of several corporations. Brian Tracy says that sales is simply "approaching each customer with the idea of helping him or her to solve a problem or achieve a goal, not of selling a product or service." That's true, and my approach to the job interview is the same as my approach to sales. So while you're reading this book, if it appears that I'm training you to be a better salesperson, I've done my job.

You probably are not formally trained in sales. Most people aren't, and they don't understand how to stand out in the crowd, to build an instant rapport, to communicate with empathy and a personal touch, and to create an emotional connection. Selling is a delicate but structured art, and if unprepared, a lot of things can go wrong. So can a job interview. But with good planning, a lot of things can go right too.

A job interview is just like a sales presentation. Interviewing is simply selling yourself, and the success of your efforts to sell yourself often comes down not to your talent and experience but how you communicate—how you sell yourself. There are some specific techniques you can employ, which I'll teach you in this book, to ensure that your presentation is more effective than most of the candidates you're competing against. I'll also

Introduction

help you avoid the typical and atypical mistakes that sink most candidates during the interview.

Realize that when you go into a job interview, almost all of the other candidates have similar backgrounds, skills, and experience; otherwise, they would not have been invited to apply. It's a level playing field. The difference is in *how* you present, not *what* you present. I'm going to show you how to present yourself better than other candidates and how to avoid the mistakes the other candidates are bound to make.

Michael Scott, a character in *The Office*, once said, "My, how the turn tables." Laughable, of course, but I want to help you turn the table and take control of your job interview. Most of the time, the interviewer is also unprepared, anxious, and probably has little or no training on how best to conduct an interview. He or she is ripe for being a turned table. By the time you finish this book, you'll understand how to be the one in the room who's the better communicator. You'll maintain control of the interview. You'll be the one who makes the decision to take the job. I guarantee that you will STAND OUT!

1

Replace Negative
Emotions with
Positive Actions

BEFORE WE LAUNCH into the practical aspects of my proven STAND OUT! strategies, we need to get your feet on the ground. By that I mean we need to give you a strong sense of calm and confidence.

> Most job interview candidates are dead on arrival simply because they are anxious and unprepared the interview.

Most job interview candidates are dead on arrival simply because they are anxious and unprepared for the interview. Have you felt that way? Your résumé, experience, education, and certifications all go out the window if you can't find a way to pull it together during the interview. Having excess anxiety will not allow you to properly and calmly communicate your value or to remember the questions you want to ask. So before we can work on preparing you for your next job interview, we need to address your emotions and negative thinking inside your head.

I've never met anyone who actually likes job interviews. They are universally despised. Walking into a job interview is literally one of the most stressful things you'll *ever* do. You might break into a cold sweat and shake like a leaf with your heart racing. You won't sleep the night (or even nights) before the interview either. Then you awkwardly brace yourself, walk into the room, and sit down in the dreaded chair opposite the interviewer's desk. The first few minutes of an interview can be the worst part because you're already so emotionally distraught, you feel that you're leaving a bad first impression, and then it all tailspins. You start imagining that you're performing worse than you actually are, and a sense of dread and panic begins to set in. The anxiety and associated depression can be overwhelming.

Don't feel bad; almost everyone feels this way. Harris Interactive recently surveyed Americans

Replace Negative Emotions with Positive Actions

about job interviews and reported that a whopping 9 out of 10 employed adults say they fear something about the experience, and nearly 30 percent are more anxious about job interviews than going to the doctor. It's enough to send your blood pressure through the roof.

When I work with my clients to help them prepare for their job interviews, I play three roles: CEO, professional sales trainer, and therapist. Yes, you read that correctly. I'm certainly not a certified or licensed counselor, but as someone who has studied human nature as it relates to buying and selling, I understand what it means and what it takes to replace negative emotions with positive. And as someone who's interviewed hundreds upon hundreds of applicants, I can see the look of dread on your face when you sit down for the interview. I feel your pain, and I want to replace the pain with gain. If you can turn the tables on your emotions, I promise you'll STAND OUT!

This chapter is central to everything else I'm going to teach you in this book. We need to boost your zen and give you calm assurance that you're going to be OK.

For a long time, I was unaware that my job interview methodologies leveraged the same scientifically proven Cognitive Behavioral Therapy (CBT) techniques used by professional counselors worldwide. I just kept asking myself, "What can I do differently to maintain more control during a job interview?" The more I learned about CBT, the more I realized I was practicing and teaching core mental health strategies.

CBT is a type of psychotherapeutic treatment that helps people identify and change destructive thought patterns that have a negative influence on their emotions and behavior. It is commonly used by therapists to treat a host of mental health issues. But you might be surprised to learn that CBT is also being successfully used in sales training because it teaches salespeople to replace their negative emotions with specific actions that generate positive emotions, thereby creating more successful sales results..

CBT focuses on changing automatic negative thoughts that can worsen depression, anxiety, and other unhealthy mood swings. A therapist would use the treatment to change your mindset by reassessing distorted and irrational thought patterns you've developed over time. Negative thoughts are identified, challenged, and replaced with more objective, realistic thoughts. You identify, tackle, and change unhelpful thinking so that your behaviors improve. In short, you learn how to take actions that promote more control of your thoughts and emotions, which gives you more control over the interview. This will make you calmer, more confident, and focused.

What I discovered is that for most people, preparing for a job interview is a lot like dealing with many other mental health challenges. Mental health conditions such as depression and anxiety take many forms:

- Thinking in black and white
- Over-generalizing
- Ignoring the positive and focusing on the negative
- Catastrophizing
- Being overwhelmed by irrational fears
- Responding with a fight-or-flight response (also known as an acute stress response)

These are a lot like the same negative thought patterns you experience going into a job interview, don't they? Some people literally go into a panic attack before a job interview. I think we've all "been there, done that" in one way or another.

Again, it's the fear of the unknown that causes the imagination to run wild with negative thoughts and emotions before and during a job interview. Your anxiety literally leads to panic or irrational fear as you falsely imagine *everything that might go wrong*. As I developed my job interview strategies and then observed how much they help individuals successfully prepare for job interviews, I realized that I was helping them replace their negative thoughts and emotions with a predetermined set of behaviors (questions) that leads to positive ones, much like a therapist does with CBT.

> Preparing for a job interview is a lot like dealing with many other mental health challenges.

I cannot overestimate how important it is to find constructive ways to reduce your anxieties related to your job interviews. Your mood before and during the interview will far outweigh anything else you say or do, including what's on your résumé. We'll explore this throughout the book. What I'll teach you will replace your fear with actions that instill and convey confidence. If you can do that, you're already ahead of most people in your sense of confidence and calm.

But to get started today, CBT therapists would tell you to:

- **Acknowledge the emotions.** Job interviewing is stressful. It's natural to be anxious and even depressed about the process. Everyone else is just as nervous as you are.
- **Identify and clarify the thought.** Pick apart the most distressing part of the job interview. Understand the implications of the way you're thinking. Treat the thought as an object.
- **Take your emotions out of the equation.** Sit back and think it through. Try to be clear and rational. Set the emotion aside, even for just a moment, and approach the interview more rationally.
- **Come at it from a different angle.** Maybe you'll recognize that the interview will teach you valuable lessons for the future, even if you don't get the job. Treat your job interview as if you're an investigative reporter.

- **Try and focus on how you can help the employer.** It's easy to get caught up in the idea of being judged as a candidate for the job, which can greatly increase anxiety. But if you stay focused on clarifying and their needs and what skills or experience you have that would help, then you will tend not to focus yourself too much.

When I coach job applicants, they come out of the process with less anxiety and more confidence simply by taking control of their negative emotions. It's not hard to do, but it does take some intentionality and purpose. Happiness is a choice!

In the next chapter, we'll look at four ways to gain control of the job interview. Your success depends largely on who's controlling the interview.

2

Gain Control of the Room

ANYTIME YOU'RE IN a conversation with another person, one of you is in control. We often think that the person in control is smarter, more experienced, louder or more passionate, but that is not always the case. Doing most of the of the talking just means that you are dominating the conversation, not controlling it necessarily.

> During a job interview, you want to be the one in control.

Verbosity isn't necessarily equivalent to intelligence, and talkativeness doesn't result in persuasion. In fact, in some job interviews, the interviewer does most of the talking, rarely even asking questions; in others, the interviewee is verbose and does most of the talking. It can go both ways, and neither way necessarily indicates who is in control. So I'm not suggesting that you be the most talkative during the interview. But I am suggesting you control the interview.

"Can I be in control if I'm the one being interviewed?" you ask. Of course you can, and in fact, I can show you how to take control in a way that will even impress the interviewer, at least on a subconscious level. I believe that in any conversation, whoever is more prepared will inevitably convey the most important information. It will come about more naturally and without effort. It doesn't mean you have to talk the most, but it does mean that you have to take control of the social construct. You have to guide the direction of the interview.

Does this sound intimidating? It doesn't need to scare you. Remember when you're being interviewed, the interviewer has insecurities just as you do. So if you can leverage that and take control of the interview, you'll be remembered for it in the interviewer's mind, and in a very positive way. I truly believe that the interviewer interprets a collaborative conversation much

Gain Control of the Room

more positively than one that is only driven by responses to questions.

There are four ways to take control of the room and master the conversation. They're quite simple if you plan ahead for it. The amazing part is that the interviewer won't even realize you had control of the interview, but he or she will realize that you're the right candidate for the job.

First, stop imagining you're the only nervous one in the room. The person sitting across the desk, the one asking the questions, is also nervous. In fact, he may be just as anxious about the interview as you are. Most managers have had very little training in performing job interviews. They often "shoot from the hip" and hope for the best. Most commonly, these have a standard set of questions they ask in every interview. (i.e...Tell me about yourself?, What's your spirit animal?, etc.) Have you ever been in a job interview where the interviewer did most of the speaking? Or hardly asked any questions at all? The reason is because he doesn't understand the best approach and is just as anxious as you are about it. During an interview, everyone in the room is anxious. It can feel very awkward. Both the interviewer and interviewee really have no idea where it's all headed. So toss out all those irrational fears related to you being the more timid one. It's altogether possible that you can quickly turn the tables by being the calmer and more reassuring person in the room.

Second, remember that you are not the only candidate being interviewed. When you're overly anxious, you begin to feel like a nervous bride walking down the aisle, knowing every single eyeball is focused squarely on you. There's even a phobia called Scopophobia that is connected with social anxiety and a few other conditions. It causes a severe fear of being stared at. You need to toss all these thoughts out the window also. The interviewer is probably meeting dozens of applicants in a single day, or even hundreds over a week's or month's time. She gets tired and remembers much less information than you think. By midday, an interviewer is often even too tired to take good notes. While you're sitting in an interview for only thirty to sixty minutes, he's sitting in interviews for up to eight hours a day. That's exhausting.

Why is it important to remember this? It will help you to stop obsessing over the little things. As a job candidate, you are on the same footing as the interviewer. You both want it to be a productive conversation and determine if there is a mutual fit.

> So before and during an interview, relax about the relationship between you and the interviewer.

The interviewer will never remember any slips or blunders because he will see and hear them all day long. So before and during an interview, relax about the relationship between you and the interviewer. If you can redirect your thoughts in this way, you may even have the upper hand. Consider the possibility that you are entering the room less anxious than the interviewer. Maybe you can impress him by bringing calm and levity to the situation. If you're the calmer person in the room, I guarantee you'll be remembered for it.

Third, try to go into an interview with a positive mindset. Part of your anxiety is due to the fact that you may feel desperate. Most of the time, you interview for jobs because you need a new one. Either you've been fired, laid off, or otherwise have lost your job. Or, for various reasons, you don't like your current job anymore. You're looking for more money or a better situation. By this time, you've already mentally and emotionally disassociated from your current job, which means you're getting desperate for a new one. Desperate people make poor choices and get trapped into panic mode. So try not to come off as desperate. Hiring managers, like all people, love it when they feel like they are just having a conversation and feels effortless. The key to having a conversation that feels effortless is that it's not solely about you.

Gain Control of the Room

Finally, go into the job interview as if you're the lead investigator of a crime. You're there to collect information, seek knowledge, and explore possibilities. This will shift the focus away from you and put yourself in the right frame of mind. You're not a criminal behind a bright light. You might feel that you are, but you aren't. You are an investigative reporter seeking information about whether or not the company or organization is the right fit for you. Make it about them, not you. You're the champion, the gold medal winner, the wearer of the blue ribbon. That much is obvious, but what's not obvious yet is: Are you a good fit? Only you can determine that. So go into the room with the attitude of the investigator, because you are really just looking to identify the next best opportunity for you, not just hoping that they pick you.

> Go into the job interview as if you're the lead investigator of a crime.

Work through these four strategies in your head before the interview, use them early on, and then don't let yourself lose control during the entire interview. Here's a great way to begin. It's commonly recommended that you ask the interviewer a question very early on, possibly something related to their office setting. "I see you have a portrait of Tiger Woods on the wall. I love golf! When was the last time you hit the golf course?" A question like this is fine, but I recommend steering the conversation toward the career of the interviewer, to better connect on a professional level. A better question might be: "I noticed that you have been here for 5 years already, what brought you to the company?" or "I noticed that there are lots of openings here. What's driving all of the change?" This gets him talking about himself in relation to the work, and it gives you a better opportunity to talk about your own career and how it might be a similar fit.

Now we'll dive into how to ask the right questions during an interview. You don't want to just become a master at answering questions, but also at asking them.

3

Setting the Stage

BEFORE I SHARE more with you about the job interview, how to prepare for it, and how to handle yourself during, I want to recommend you do something that very few candidates ever consider doing.

Most of us think that the job interview begins when we sit down and begin to speak with the hiring manager, either in-person or by video. But this couldn't be further from the truth. Days or even weeks before the actual job interview begins, you can begin to become the lead candidate and establish control over the hiring process. How so? In this chapter I'm going to show you how to reach out and start the job

> Days or even weeks before the actual job interview begins, you can begin to become the lead candidate and establish control over the hiring process.

interview even before the interview begins. Very few job candidates attempt to reach out to hiring managers before the interview begins. But when you do, you jump right to the head of the pack.

How can you do this, you ask?

Well, imagine that you are told that you have been selected to interview for a position, either through a recruiter or by someone in a Human Resource department. Once this step has occurred, you can now establish a connection with the interviewer(s) by reaching out to them directly to confirm the date/time of the interview and set the agenda. Yes, you can actually set the agenda, and by doing so you are conveying to the interviewer that you are organized and that you plan ahead. Would you say those are important qualities that employers are looking for? Absolutely!

> You can actually set the agenda, and by doing so you are conveying to the interviewer that you are organized and that you plan ahead.

Setting the Stage

At this point, I know what you're thinking. You think that this might be too aggressive or otherwise offensive, to reach out and contact the hiring manager before the interview even begins. But try not to be timid or bashful, and imagine the tables were turned. If you were doing the interviewing and someone reached out to you beforehand, you'd certainly remember that person, right? And when the interview actually begins, would you have a more positive or negative impression of that person? I think we'd all agree it would be more positive, give the pre-interview communication was done with professionalism.

Here is one example of how this is done with tact and professionalism:

Send the following email or a phone call each person you are interviewing with:

Good morning, Tim!
I was just informed that we have a meeting on November 9th at 2pm EST. I wanted to confirm our appointment and also share my goals for our

upcoming discussion, which I'm looking forward to.

My goals for our time together as are as follows:

- *Provide you with an overview of my background and career objectives.*
- *Learn more about ACME's 1-3 year growth strategy.*
- *Clarify responsibilities for this role and how they will contribute to your strategy.*

Please let me know if you have any additional goals for our meeting as well. I look forward to our discussion and determining if there is a mutual fit.

Sincerely,
Tony Caputo

This email should be sent as soon as you are informed of the time and date of your upcoming interview. Now let's analyze some of the reasons

Setting the Stage

why this step is so important to make you STAND OUT.

First, it establishes that fact that you are someone who knows how to set targets and manage your activities to achieve those targets. This is rare among job candidates.

> After going out of your way to establish genuine interest, I guarantee the interview will go in a different direction.

Second, you are setting an expectation for having a real discussion versus an interview. It might sound like a minor detail, but it matters a lot more than you think.

Third, you are giving the interviewer the opportunity to establish additional goals and objectives for the meeting. This demonstrates a level of professional courtesy.

Fourth, you are demonstrating leadership behavior, and also good salesmanship. If you're interviewing for a job that entails communication with customers in any way, this proves you're good at it.

Very few of the other candidates (likely none) will take these additional steps. They show up blindly at the interview and hope for the best. But if you reach out beforehand and begin communication, you're already halfway there. The interviewer knows you and has some context to begin the interview. After going out of your way to establish genuine interest, I guarantee the interview will go in a different direction. It will be more like a second interview than a first.

4

How to Ask the Right Questions

THE LAST THING you want to do in a job interview is to answer the interviewer's questions without also asking any of your own. Even if you do a great job of answering questions but then ask none, you're going to leave the interview with a less than average impression. The power of asking questions during an interview cannot be understated.

> The power of asking questions during an interview cannot be understated.

Based on the feedback I receive from many employers, you'd be surprised how many people don't ask questions at all *during* an interview. To make matters worse, the most commonly asked questions relate to compensation, benefits, or other company policies and procedures. And most often these questions are asked near the end of the interview, which is the wrong time. Let's explore this further.

First, why is it important to ask questions?

An inquisitive mind is an emotionally intelligent mind. People who have the ability to ask good questions are literally perceived to be smarter. If you sit still and silent during an interview and don't ask any inquisitive questions, the interviewer is left wondering what you're thinking or even if you care. But if you freely ask questions, it implies that you're thinking about the opportunity at a deeper level.

This isn't just theory. The Harvard Business School researched this and concluded that asking for advice makes people think you're smarter. Why so? "Ultimately, being asked for advice is flattering. It implies, as the questioner, you think the person you're asking is smart. Conversely, they'll think you're smart, because you're being proactive in completing the task to the best of your ability," writes Harvard researcher Wood Brooks.

How to Ask the Right Questions

Beyond making you appear more intelligent and plugged in, asking someone to share his experiences, insight, or passions also causes an instant connection and often even fondness. It's a powerful foundation for building fast rapport in relationships. Questions make people more likeable, and you definitely want to be a likeable person during an interview. When you ask a question, you're asking for engagement. The ensuing conversation is something an interviewer will remember. Rather than just asking questions and taking notes, the interview senses the beginning of a relationship, which will be more memorable.

What kinds of questions should you ask?

What's most important to remember is that you can ask any questions. Don't fool yourself into thinking your questions have to be the perfect pitch. We fear asking questions more proactively because we feel it would be a sign of disrespect. But being willing to ask even "dumb" questions is, ironically, one of the smartest things you can do during an interview. It's not a sign of weakness to admit that you don't have all the answers—no one does. You'll come across as more authentic and confident if you ask good questions.

I like what Dale Carnegie said almost a century ago in his notable self-help book, *How to Win Friends and Influence People*: "Ask questions the other person will enjoy answering." Indeed, people love being asked to talk about what they love.

> It's not a sign of weakness to admit that you don't have all the answers—no one does.

When you ask a question, you want to draw the interviewer into a conversation about himself and about his own experiences at the company. In this way, you will become more vested in the interview. People naturally love to talk about themselves, and the interviewer will appreciate being able to express themselves to you. If you can get him talking about his work and his own experiences at the company, you've gone a long way toward creating a bond. It will also help you better understand more about the position and the company itself.

When is the best time to ask questions during an interview?

The biggest mistake you can make is to wait until the end of an interview to start asking your questions. By that time, the interview itself has probably run out of steam. The interviewer and the interviewee are both tired, and in fact, the interviewer has probably already decided if you're a good fit or not. It's likely too late to begin to engage in questions.

Avoid telegraphing your questions. Remember you're going into the interview like an investigative reporter. But don't treat it like an interrogation. Be warm, friendly, and serious, but at the same time, be conversational. Integrate your questions during the interview. Try to fit your own questions in between answering questions. But be natural, just as you would in any other conversation. When you're talking with a friend, you don't wait until the end of the conversation to ask questions, right? Likewise, during an interview, ask questions when they'd naturally be asked.

I've developed some questions that often work well during interviews. But don't memorize these! Use them as a launch pad for questions you'd truly want to explore:

- How would you describe the culture here?
- Can you tell me what brought you to [company name], Theresa?
- John, what would you say are the company's core strengths?
- How long have you been with the company, Bob?
- Has your role changed since you've been here?
- What capabilities are most important for success in this role, Susan?
- Why did you join [company name], Blair?

- What's your favorite part about working here?
- What's one challenge you occasionally or regularly face in your job?
- Allen, as you think about the employees that are the most successful here, what are some of the qualities they have in common?
- Heather, what would you say are the company's primary growth initiatives this year?

Very few interview candidates ask good questions. In my experience, only one out of ten people will ask anything beyond basic questions about compensation or benefits. I guarantee you will STAND OUT! if you ask some engaging, intelligent, and curious questions during the interview. You will be remembered for it.

5

Align Strengths with Needs

WHY DO EMPLOYERS interview multiple candidates for each job opening? Why not just choose the best résumé? The purpose of a job interview is to not only find a new employee, but also to find someone who most closely aligns to the company's current needs. During an interview, the candidate who is perceived to be the most aligned is the one who will STAND OUT!

So now we'll explore how you can discover the company's unmet needs during the interview, and also prove to the interviewer that you're the best person to meet those needs.

It's easier to highlight your strengths and skills when a need is put on the table or discovered during an interview. If you don't know what specific problems or challenges the interviewer has in mind, it doesn't matter how much you shine in other areas. This is a critical part of my STAND OUT methodology and strategies. Those who "apply it" are usually at the head of the pack when decision-making time arrives.

A common interview question is: *Why do you want to work here?* Of all the interview questions you prepare for, the most obvious ones sometimes get the least attention. Yes, you came ready to share your biggest flaw, your greatest strength, or a moment when you shined, but sometimes the toughest job interview question is simple and direct. "Why do you want to work here?" is a tough one. It requires that you focus on a specific answer without any context or prompt from the interviewer. It's a blank space and an open slate.

The reason you're being asked this common question is so the interviewer can dig a little deeper into how you might align with the company's current needs. While an interviewer is hiring you for who you are and what you can do, she usually has some specific outcomes in mind. There are specific challenges at hand, particular problem areas that need to be addressed, and a specific project (or projects) that will need your attention. A job description is not simply "what you see is what you get." Hidden between the lines are challenges that need to be met. The interviewer is looking for someone who might best meet those challenges.

> A job description is not simply "what you see is what you get."

For example, a job description might say that part of your role will be to "manage the company's social media marketing campaigns." But there might be deeper problems under the hood. The previous employee may have left the company in a lurch and in a mess, or the company may have had bad experiences in the past with social media. Even more problematic, expectations for social media success may be significantly unrealistic. These are just examples, but as you might imagine, there are always a plethora of problems within every company. Your job during the interview is to uncover these, so that you can prioritize your strengths according to what the interviewer shares about these challenges.

Again, we're not talking about the company's mission, values, history, latest investor reports, or financial statements. While these are also important to research and understand going into the interview, they won't help you get into the mind of the interviewer to better understand exactly what and where the real problems are.

There are three ways you can try to pry open the door with the interviewer.

First, and very simply, you want to highlight the challenge at hand. So ask direct questions about the kinds of problems the company is currently facing in reference to the job you are interviewing for. While this might seem like a pushy or otherwise overly forward question, the interviewer will probably appreciate the opportunity to talk about it. I promise you, it will show that you care (more than those who don't ask the question).

Examples might be:

Align Strengths with Needs

- What have historically been the most challenging aspects of this role?
- What skill sets would you say are the most important for success in this role?
- How will my performance in this role be measured?

Second, share how you approached a similar problem in a previous role. And don't wait to be asked. Volunteer the information before the conversation gets away from both you and the interviewer. This might be a challenging extemporaneous exercise because you've just entered new territory in the interview. Going into the interview, there is no way you can research something that hasn't been previously disclosed. But try to relax and think quickly on your feet. If you can share a scenario that's even remotely

> Going into the interview, there is no way you can research something that hasn't been previously disclosed.

close, you're doing better than most by simply volunteering that you're acquainted with a similar situation.

Finally, in follow-up, share the result of the outcome. It's best to find quantifiable ways you helped address and alleviate the problem. Sometimes the results are financial, but not always. There are many ways to quantify an outcome. Here are some examples:

- By implementing a new quarterly business review with customers, our customer satisfaction and retention increased by 15 percent in a 12-month period.
- Launching that new digital marketing program increased the number of new leads by 38 percent over the next 6 months.
- As a result of the new account collection strategy, our 13-week cash flow improved by 32 percent.

Align Strengths with Needs

Again, during an interview, you want to align *your specific strengths* with the *company's specific needs*. If you can do this effectively, you'll be yards ahead of where most people are during an interview. In my experience, and in the experience of most employers I've worked with, candidates rarely go beyond basic company research. Also make sure to confirm that you've provided enough detail before the interview ends. Be upfront and sincere with the interviewer by asking, "Did I give you enough information?" or "Is there anything else you'd like to know about how I approached this?"

> During an interview, you want to align *your specific strengths* with the *company's specific needs.*

Alignment is an important goal during an interview, and so is being likeable. Next I'll share the importance of your personality during the job interview.

6

The Likeability Factor

WE ALL LIKE to work with pleasant, genuine, and fun people. Some people are so much fun to work with that you actually look forward to seeing their faces come Monday morning. And others? Frankly, you wish they worked somewhere else. During a job interview, you want to be the person that people love to work with!

> During a job interview, you want to be the person that people love to work with!

Being likeable is probably the most overlooked and under-discussed part of the interview process. You can have a sterling résumé, solid education and experience, and the best answers to the toughest questions, but if you're not likeable, chances are you won't get hired. Being likeable is one of the great intangibles that managers seek. Hiring managers are only human. They want to like the person that they'll spend over eight hours a day with. It might fly in the face of fairness, but if the tables were turned, you'd also prefer to hire someone you liked.

Don't underestimate the likeability factor! Personality is what will make you stand out and be remembered. Some people are naturally fun, interesting, and extroverted. We all know someone who is the "life of the party." But most of us need a little help in this area. How can you come across more likeable during an interview?

First, watch your body language. Make eye contact with the interviewer, but don't linger for too long or it will become uncomfortable. For some of us, eye contact is uncomfortable, but I cannot express how important this is. Don't let your eyes wander around the room too much. Relax, look eye-to-eye, and smile. A funny thing about eye contact is if it's too little, you will seem tentative, but if it's too much, you might seem creepy. Go for the middle ground. And every once in a while, nod your head to show that you're paying attention.

You need to be cognizant of your other body language also. You want to demonstrate warmth and openness. Try not to sit stiffly with your arms crossed over your chest. Don't squirm or fidget in your seat. Don't ever sigh, roll your eyes, or rudely interrupt the person mid-speech. Avoid looking at your watch, and by any and all means, never look at your phone. Imagine you're sitting with an old friend and be your genuine self. It's easy being genuine with an old friend, right?

Second, always stay positive and upbeat in your language and mannerisms. Avoid saying anything negative about past companies you worked for, previous co-workers or bosses, or anything else for that matter. You want your potential employer to think you have unending enthusiasm and persistence. This is not to say you should come across in a fake way. Be yourself, but be your happy, positive self. If you do this, you will portray yourself as someone who is not desperate for the job. Happy people are confident and comfortable in their own shoes.

Third, and this is not necessarily easy, try to mimic the interviewer's speed, pace, and tone. In psychology, this is called "mirroring." Mirroring is a nonverbal technique in which a person copies the body language, vocal qualities, or attitude of someone else. It occurs throughout all of your social interaction and often goes unnoticed. You do it all the time. During an interview, try to be more conscious about it. If the interview speaks quietly, speak quietly. If the interviewer speaks slowly, answer slowly. If the interviewer laughs a lot, try to chuckle along. If possible, however, try to speak a little faster than you normally do, but of course still be natural. When you mirror the other person during an interview, you'll build faster rapport when it's perceived that you're aligned with them personally.

> Every time you use someone's name, that person feels important.

Fourth—and you might be surprised how important this is—use the interviewer's name. Every time you use someone's name, that person feels important. He feels that he has a little more connection with you. He listens to what you have to say, and it makes the interviewer feel more comfortable. Think about some of the most charismatic people you know. Often, when someone we think of as "charismatic" enters a room of strangers, the first thing he'll do is ask them what their names are. And after he says someone's name, he'll repeat it often. Make it a point to use the interviewer's name at the beginning and end of the interview while making eye contact. Then use it at least a few other times during the interview. Don't forget to smile when you say their name!

Lastly, but most importantly, be engaging and conversational while you ask the interviewer about his work and life. Your goal during the interview isn't just to provide good answers, but to ask good questions about the interviewer and their perspective. There's an old joke: "Enough about me; now let's talk about me." That's funny and also true.

Say you're at a party and you strike up a conversation with someone you've never met before. He tells you a funny story. It's a pretty good story, so you ask questions about details and specifics, allowing the person to talk about himself even more. After you part ways, who made the better first impression—the person who told the funny story or the one who took more of an interest in the story by asking questions?

Even science backs up the notion that talking about yourself may not actually be the most effective strategy for selling yourself. New research from a team of Harvard psychological scientists suggests that asking more questions—and in particular, asking more follow-up questions—increases people's positive impressions. "Whereas prior data demonstrate that people tend to talk about themselves [during an interview], our results suggest this may not be an optimal strategy," writes lead researcher Karen Huang and colleagues. "Instead, across several studies, we find a positive relationship between question-asking and liking."

Do you need some help asking good questions about the interviewer's work and life? Here are some examples that will help focus the interview not on you, but on the interviewer:

- So, Jim, what brought you to the company?
- How would you describe the onboarding process here at [company name], Susan?
- What are some of the things that you noticed were different about [company name] when you first joined, Larry?
- What the number one reason that you personally value the culture here at [company name]?
- What do the most valuable employees here at [company name] have in common?

When the interviewer likes you, you quickly go to the top of the pile. In some cases, for some interviewers, likeability is actually the most important quality they are looking for, even if subconsciously. Now let's jump into the number one most asked interview question, and how you should answer it.

7

Tell Me About Yourself

IF YOU'RE NOT ready for this question, then you're definitely not ready for a job interview. "Tell me about yourself" is asked by more than 90 percent of the job interviewers I've surveyed. Yet many job seekers don't take it very seriously. Indeed, it's usually asked casually and without much intent, and it's a somewhat lazy approach to launching into an interview. But it's a great opportunity for you to jump out of the gate strong.

I don't usually recommend scripting out an answer for any job interview question because memorized answers can come across as rigid or too rehearsed. But since this open-ended question is bound to be asked, it's a great opportunity for you to answer it with clarity and confidence. This is your chance to STAND OUT! early on in the interview, since it's also usually the first question asked. Your answer, and the way you answer it, will also say a lot about your confidence. As an open-ended question, it shows how you react to open-ended situations. If you stumble here, the interviewer is going to worry that you're not "good on your feet." If you shine, the interviewer will be impressed by your ability to handle yourself well under pressure.

So let's dig into this one, and you can get busy crafting out your answer, memorizing it, or at least going into the interview with a very good idea as to how you're going to answer. You might tailor your answer based on the specific job description, the company, or the interviewer, but all the same, you need to be fully equipped to answer it without having to think about it. It should roll off your tongue.

First, this is your opportunity to talk about yourself personally, not professionally. Why is this important? Interviewers shy away from personal questions. The potential for liability at the interview stage in the hiring process is tremendous. Under the Civil Rights Act of 1964 and other federal and state laws, it's illegal to discriminate against applicants on the basis of race, color, sex, religion, national origin, citizenship, disability, and age. Some states also have more protected categories, such as sexual orientation and marital status. Consequently, any question—regardless of the interviewer's intent—on any of those topics should be avoided to ensure that an inference of discrimination isn't raised when an applicant is rejected. Even a stray comment by the interviewer that offends an applicant can spell big trouble for an employer.

But interviewers desperately want to know more about your personal life. That's why they scour social media looking for more information about you. Your personal life probably tells the interview more about the kind of worker you are than anything else you might say about your past work experiences. So use this question as a way to let the interviewer into your personal life. You don't need to divulge anything you're not comfortable talking about, and you should avoid talking about personal relationships (dating, for example), but this is a good time to talk about who you are as a person.

For example, you might want to talk about your family background. Telling the interviewer where and how you grew up is always an interesting place to start. It gives a little context as to who you are. Then possibly talk about why you reside where you do today and what brought you there. Discussions about geography are always interesting and usually lead to engaging conversation about "people and places."

During an interview, I often explain that I come from a military family. This usually implies that I was raised in a disciplined or structured environment, which can be a positive, depending on the role and the perception of the interviewer. Think about something from your personal background that will be perceived as a strength, particularly for the specific position you're interviewing for. For example, let's say you are interviewing for a medical position. You might say something like this: "My father was a doctor, so I was raised in a home where we discussed health and medicine on a regular basis."

Then it's usually helpful to share some details about a hobby or other leisure activity that you enjoy. Having hobbies and interests outside of the workplace allows you to share your passions and become a healthier and more well-rounded person. Hiring managers ask this question to know if you have avenues to de-stress outside of work and to better understand what makes you happy. Have fun with this question as your enthusiasm will surely infect the interviewer. But don't overkill it. Keep the description of your hobby or interest fairly brief unless your interviewer asks you to elaborate. Then, if possible, make it clear how your extracurricular activities make you a good fit for the company in terms of your values or passions. And hobbies can also be fun activities you enjoy such as attending concerts or movies, watching NFL football, or taking nature walks. Share anything that helps portray you as an interesting person to work with.

This is also a good place to share more about your education. Education doesn't come up in an interview as often as you'd think. Interviewers primarily want to know if you have a degree in a specified area, but beyond that, not many will ask questions. So take this opportunity to share more about your school, why you chose it, and what made your educational experiences unique or relevant to the role. This is especially helpful if you attended a lesser-known school, or if you studied in an area that is different from the role you're interviewing for (which is very common).

> Share anything that helps portray you as an interesting person to work with.

You want the interviewer to understand that your educational experience was beneficial in some way and that you worked hard during your time in college or a university. So avoid saying anything else contrary. Don't say, "Well, I learned how to hold my beer, that's for sure. The partying was fun, but now it's time to get serious." Also, try to express some real world connections between your academic studies and the job you're applying for. Focus on the real world applications of your education. And if you have had work experience and/or internships, this is an opportunity to talk specifically about what you learned in the classroom that helped you in your work. Overall, you want to discuss your education briefly but with intention and with a positive attitude. Make it clear that your educational journey was beneficial and that you are just as excited to keep learning.

Finally, once you've shared something about yourself, who you are, what you like to do, and your education, say something high-level about your work. Don't spend time here getting into the nitty-gritty about your work experiences, but instead share a macro look of why you love your work, what made you decide to do this, why it excites you, and how you much you're looking forward to continue expanding your horizons. This is a good time and place to give the interviewer a more broad-based understanding of who you are related to your profession.

To be sure, when you "tell about yourself," you want to be perceived as an interesting, optimistic person who has real-life connections to the work itself. Remember that part of your job during an interview is to explore for yourself whether or not you're the right fit. You don't want to take a job you'll end up hating. You're an investigative journalist who is sharing details about your life to solicit feedback from the interviewer. You want to control every aspect of the job interview, including the most common question: Tell me about yourself.

If you can master and answer this one very important question, you'll STAND OUT! There are also some questions you should simply not answer, which we'll review next.

8

Questions You Should Never Answer

IN THE UNITED States, it is illegal for an employer to discriminate against a job applicant because of race, color, religion, sex (including gender identity, sexual orientation, and pregnancy), age, national origin, or disability. We reviewed this in a previous chapter. Such questions seldom arise, however, when they do it can make it awkward for the interview to continue. If you're asked any of these questions, you might feel as if the rug is being pulled out from under you. In this chapter, we'll look at how to best handle potentially illegal, unethical, or awkward questions.

Every once in a while, an interviewer will ask personal questions that are inappropriate, illegal, and that ought not to be answered. If you feel that the interviewer is asking such questions with malice, your best option may be to politely end the interview and seek guidance from an employment attorney. The law strictly prohibits the interviewer from asking certain questions. Under no circumstance are you required to answer.

But also, don't always assume the worst. The interviewer may be naïve, untrained, too casual, or simply trying to get to know you better. You'd be surprised at how complex the law really is.

For example, it's **illegal** to ask:

Are you married? Do you have children? If so, what do you do for child care?

But it's **legal** to ask:

Do you have any obligations that would prevent you from working overtime, traveling, or relocating?

It's **illegal** to ask:

What is your religion?

But it's **legal** to ask:

Can you work on Sundays?

So it's not as cut-and-dried as you might think it is. During an interview, questions may arise that the interviewer literally didn't know was illegal. Or the interviewer was confused, but I would suggest that you assume best intentions. Finally, it's also possible that the interviewer is savvy enough to ask certain illegal questions in a legal way. For example, "Where were you born?" is illegal, but "Where in the country did you grow up?" is legal.

I always suggest there are three options for job seekers who are confronted with awkward personal questions:

First, you might want to side-step the question. You can politely refuse to answer the question but address the core concern. For example, if your interviewer asks whether or not you have children, he or she might really be concerned about whether your family responsibilities might interfere with company travel. You could respond by saying, "I have made arrangements to cover my childcare needs when I travel and it will not interfere with my professional responsibilities." For certain, always avoid volunteering information about your spouse or children. It may subconsciously bias the interview. Also avoid talking about getting married or having children in the future for the same reasons.

Second, question the relevance of the question in the first place. You want to do this with tact and a quiet tone, but also firmness. You can ask your interviewer how the question relates to the position you're interviewing for. This may alert him to the inappropriate nature of their question. Again, the interviewer might be naïve or too friendly. But if you feel that he is asking an inappropriate or discriminatory question, you can refuse to answer the question and try changing the subject, or you may choose to excuse yourself from the interview. This is an entirely appropriate option, and you should not feel bad about it. Retain your dignity, be polite, and simply walk out of the room. But consider digging a little deeper and try to explore the relevance of the question in the first place.

Third, you might want to answer the question. If you think the interviewer was simply trying to get to know you and naïvely asked the question, you can of course choose to answer. Again, try to consider the intent of the question. For example, was the interviewer asking about your birthplace because he or she grew up in the same area and is trying to get to know you? If you are comfortable answering, then it's fine to do so.

Questions about your personal life are often unnecessary today due to social media. According to a survey by CareerBuilder, a full 70 percent of employers "use social media to screen candidates before hiring." That means even before you walk through the door, the interviewer is likely to know a lot about you. He doesn't need to ask if you're married, have children, go to the beach, or have an opinion about politics or religion. Everything is laid bare on Facebook, Instagram, Twitter, LinkedIn, and even, of course, Google. So before you go into an interview, look at your social media feeds and think about them from the perspective of the job interviewer. Every illegal question that could be asked is probably answered on your social media accounts.

As it turns out, those personal details are precisely why recruiters and hiring managers keep tabs on applicants' social media accounts. It can help them get a more accurate idea about who you are outside of your résumé. A résumé can tell about your qualifications, but your social media profile can help determine your personality type and if you're a good fit for the corporate culture. Plus, recruiters are looking for red flags—risqué

> So before you go into an interview, look at your social media feeds and think about them from the perspective of the job interviewer.

photos, bad language, signs of drug use—that would show them you'd be a less than ideal person to have on the staff.

How does this impact the interview? How should you deal with it? For example, if your social media feed includes posts about your recent engagement to be married or about having a baby, you might offer the information during the interview as a way to dissuade the interviewer from shying away from you as a potential candidate. If your social media feeds are filled with such posts, you should assume the interviewer already knows about it. So it might be a good time and place to talk about it.

Are there also questions you should avoid asking? Certainly! Next, we'll talk about questions you should avoid asking so you will STAND OUT!

9

Questions You Should Avoid Asking

I ALWAYS ENCOURAGE applicants to ask questions, sometimes lots of questions, during a job interview. But there are certain questions you want to avoid. The order in which you ask them is equally as important. My STAND OUT! methodology requires you to ask questions, but if you ask the wrong ones, or the right ones at the wrong time, you might increase your odds of getting passed over.

> Remember, when you first sit down for a job interview, you're a blank slate.

Remember, when you first sit down for a job interview, you're a blank slate. The interviewer knows nothing about you aside from what he's read about you on your résumé. He has no context for who you are, what you're like, and whether or not you'd be a good fit for the company and position. For all practical purposes, you're a complete stranger. This is very important to keep in mind if and when you pose your questions during the interview.

For example, if you pose self-serving questions too early, you'll appear, well, self-serving. You haven't even built up enough of a rapport yet. By self-serving, I'm referring to questions about compensation and benefits, or such details as your office, your assistant, or vacation time. A job interview is a two-way street. The potential employer asks questions to determine if you're an ideal fit for the job, and your job during the interview is to assess the same. Before you can dig into your compensation, you need to establish your alignment with the needs of the business and your value with the hiring manager. You need to make the interview about them, not you. And you need to do some discovery to determine if this is the kind of job you'll succeed in. If you ask probing questions too early about compensation and benefits, the interview effectively ends there.

Questions You Should Avoid Asking

It's almost always best to wait until the end of the interview to ask these questions. Even then, you might just want to avoid asking them altogether. If you're asked to come in for a second interview, or if you're offered the position, then you'll have plenty of time to ask questions about your compensation and fringe benefits. Why even ask these questions during the interview? There's almost no good reason, ever. If you want to STAND OUT, move on and worry about it after you have an offer in your hand.

> Avoid asking for information you could have easily found in your research.

There are other questions you should avoid asking altogether.

Avoid asking for information you could have easily found in your research. Anyone can easily do a quick web search and discover who a company's owner is, how much revenue they're bringing in annually assuming they are a public company, almost anything about the company's products and services, and even who key leaders and staff members are. If you dig a little deeper, you can discover a lot more about a company, even details the company may wish you didn't know. While it's vitally important you do your research, hold your cards close to your chest. If you ask a question that is readily available on the Internet, it may make you look more foolish and less wise.

Avoid asking about future promotions. This is a tricky one, but asking about future promotions might mean to the hiring manager that you're not interested in the job you're actually interviewing for. He may question himself, "This person hasn't even been hired yet but is already focused on being promoted?" On the other hand, companies attract competitive candidates by offering growth opportunities. They may even highlight efforts to help employees grow and evolve through professional development, education, or promotions.

Since "growth" can be a code word for future promotions, asking this question not in a self-serving way, but in context of the company's values. That's a safer way to ask the question.

Other questions you should avoid asking:

- Never ask about background or drug testing but assume they will likely require these types of assessments.
- Never ask if the company monitors emails or Internet usage. Most companies do whether you know if or not.
- Never ask if you'll have an office or an assistant.
- Never ask about politics, even if it appears you're on the "same side."

Again, some of this might seem obvious to you. But you'd be shocked at how many people stumble through interviews by asking bad questions. At the beginning of this book, I shared how you should approach the interview with calmness and less anxiety. If you simply follow my methodology in this book, including in this chapter, you can relax with confidence that you're going to STAND OUT!

10

How to Talk About Your Education

JAISON ABEL AND Richard Dietz of the Federal Reserve Bank of New York researched careers as they relate to college degrees. It may surprise you to learn that a vast majority of U.S. college graduates work in jobs that aren't related to their degrees. In fact, only about 27 percent of all Americans work in fields that are related to their degrees. Most have found jobs elsewhere and never again work in the areas in which they were originally educated.

What does this mean for the job interview? When you're asked about your education, chances are you weren't educated for the job you're applying for. This can become a stumbling block if you're not prepared for it. But I consider questions about education to be one of the best ways to STAND OUT! during the interview process, namely because most people stumble around it.

Before we get into that, many people do seek jobs in the same fields in which they earned a degree. You might be one of them. If that is the case, you're one step ahead of the competition. This is your chance to talk specifically about how your education puts you on the top of the pile. You will want to share the coursework you completed, professors who mentored you, honors and awards you may have received, and any other relevant special academic achievements. You might also boast a bit that you're doing what you were originally "called" to do or why you have a deep interest in this area of work. This will certainly impress the hiring manager.

But if you went to college to study English literature, and now you're interviewing for a job in marketing, you need to take this opportunity to tell your story. This is one of the best times during an interview to share more about who you are, to talk about your journey of professional development, and to share your goals and aspirations. This is where you tell the interviewer that your education, albeit important, pales in comparison to how much you have learned in your previous positions.

Be honest with the interviewer. Explain why you chose the college or university you attended. Then explain why you chose your particular coursework and the major you invested your time in during college. This is an opportunity to talk about what you learned about yourself during this time. Take accountability for it, and share what you learned that will help you in the job you're interviewing for. This will show a lot of maturity, and the interviewer will be impressed that you thoughtfully considered how to answer questions about your education. Rather than saying very little and being embarrassed that you left the career you once hoped for, you should be proud of your

> This is an opportunity to talk about what you learned about yourself during this time.

professional journey and glad for the education you received.

You also want to clearly explain that your education helped you with critical thinking and problem solving, clear and succinct verbal communication, passion and a sense of purpose, and self-initiative. It doesn't matter what you majored in; hiring managers are looking for smart employees they can train. You'd be surprised at how little they care about your major and how much they care about what you learned and how you learn.

Next I will share a rarely used but valuable technique that will cause the hiring manager to remember you over other candidates. Remember that interviewers often talk to dozens and even hundreds of candidates. Sometimes you'll be remembered for simple little things that no other candidate is doing.

11

Getting Personal without Getting Personal

JOB INTERVIEWS ARE almost always awkward and formal. Each party cautiously proceeds through the interview avoiding missteps and mistakes. Even the hiring manager is often clumsy. Unlike mixers or luncheons, interviews are uptight and impersonal experiences. So to STAND OUT, your role going into an interview is to make it more personal. You can do this by getting personal without getting personal. Let me explain.

You've heard the expression "people person," right? We use that to describe someone who enjoys being with or talking to other people. They are open, relaxed, and fun to be around. During a job interview, you want to be a people person, and in this chapter I'm going to share how you can achieve that, even if you're introverted and generally not the life of the party.

It's not hard, and it doesn't mean that you have to volunteer personal information or pretend to be the interviewer's best friend. But it does mean you should stand out as someone who's not afraid to be yourself, and you are not a robot who answers questions with clarity yet never shows your personal side. And it's not what you say but *how you say it* that can make the biggest impact. If you want to STAND OUT, you've got to find a way to be warm and friendly in the environment. Conference rooms and offices are not necessarily warm places. They can be cold and intimidating. So try harder than normal to be the opposite. Be warm, engaging, and happy (yes, happy!).

> Be warm, engaging, and happy (yes, happy!).

How can you be more personable? There are three ways you can warm up to the hiring manager during an interview.

First, be honest and don't be afraid to be YOU. I can't tell you how many times I've sat through interviews where the candidate was stiff and clearly afraid of being himself or herself. Loosen up and pay attention to your body language. Approach the interview like a conversation with an old friend, not an interrogation with the enemy. The person on the other side of the desk is a person just like you. Treat him that way. This doesn't mean you should come across as too casual or laid back, but it does mean that you should be relaxed, friendly, and talk like a real person. Worry less about saying the wrong thing and worry more about not saying enough.

Second, be aware that the types of questions you ask during the interview say a lot about you. If you ask introspective questions, for example, you will come across as an introspective person. If you ask very detailed questions about minutiae, you'll be seen as a person who cares a lot about details. If you ask questions about staff and human resources, you'll be perceived as a person who cares about people. See the difference? Before going into an interview, ask yourself what kind of person you're going to be. Of course, you want to be naturally YOU, but at the same time, be aware that you'll be judged by the types of questions you ask.

Third, be gracious. Try to be obviously grateful for the interview opportunity, thanking the hiring manager for his time at the beginning and the end of the interview. David Steindl-Rast, in his Ted Talk on happiness, proposes this question: "Does happiness cause one to be grateful or does being grateful create happiness?" He concludes his talk by explaining that gratitude is the sole creator of happiness. Remember the interviewer is probably more anxious, more exhausted, and certainly more confused than you are. It's a lot of work interviewing candidate after candidate. A hearty "thank you!" will go a long

> A hearty "thank you!" will go a long way toward making yourself more personal than the other candidates.

way toward making yourself more personal than the other candidates.

12

What About Your Attire?

AS A PROFESSIONAL sales trainer, I've learned that you don't get a second chance to make a good first impression. In spite of the congeniality of a job interview, you're being judged in the first few seconds, and an overall impression is formed before you even have time to sit down and get comfortable in your chair. You'd probably be surprised at how quickly some people make even *final* decisions based on a first impression. As soon as one sees another person, an impression is formed. This happens so quickly—just a fraction of a second—and what we see can sometimes dominate what we know.

Substantial research has affirmed the importance of first impressions. Researchers out of Princeton University have found that people make judgments about such characteristics as trustworthiness, competence, and likeability within a *fraction of a second* after meeting someone. They concluded that "we decide very quickly whether a person possesses many of the traits we feel are important, such as likeability and competence, even though we have not exchanged a single word with them. It appears that we are hard-wired to draw these inferences in a fast, unreflective way."

What does this mean for you as you go into an interview? Your appearance is paramount. If you're going to STAND OUT, you should pay very special attention to your attire, including your hair, jewelry, makeup, and anything else the hiring manager will observe about your appearance. Like it or not, it makes a big difference. I see far too many job candidates who take their appearance too lightly, especially these days when video interviews are so common.

> I see far too many job candidates who take their appearance too lightly, especially these days when video interviews are so common.

What About Your Attire?

A good rule of thumb is that it's always safer to show up overdressed than underdressed. While it may be appropriate to dress more casually for a second interview, you should still dress professionally then also. It's much better to be too dressed up than too casual. Dressing professionally reflects the best version of you, and it shows respect for the interviewer and the company. You may not have to dress like this every day, but you are more likely to be taken seriously when you present yourself in a professional manner and take the time to attend to details. Even your shoes should be well-polished and in good condition, not scuffed or run down at the heels.

Here are some recommendations:

- Dress in a manner that is professionally appropriate for the position for which you are applying. In many cases, this means wearing a suit jacket or dress/skirt at a minimum. When in doubt, go conservative. A dark-colored suit with

light-colored shirt is your best option. Ties are optional for the most part these days.
- Your clothes should be comfortable and fit you well so that you look and and feel confident. Anything too tight, too short or sheer be avoided.
- Avoid clothing that you would wear to a dance club.
- Clothing should be neat, clean, and pressed. Avoid wearing cologne/perfume or aftershave. You don't want to smell overpowering or worse, cause an allergic reaction.
- Make sure you have fresh breath and try to avoid eating before the interview. Don't smoke right before an interview.
- Having a recent hair cut is always a good idea.
- Makeup and nail polish should be understated; shades that are neutral to your skin tone are generally less distracting.

What About Your Attire?

The goal is to not distract the interviewer unncessarily.

- Keep your jewelry and hair accessories to a minimum, and stick to those that are not flashy, distracting, or shiny.
- Shoes should be conservative and fairly low heeled. They should be in reasonably good condition, not scuffed or run down at the heels.

All this being said, one of the biggest mistakes people can make is to apply a "one-size-fits-all" approach to attire and appearance in a job interview. Not every company culture is the same, and in some industries today, nobody dresses conservatively or wears a suit. So do your research and study up on the company culture so that you understand your audience, and play within that space. While wearing a suit or other formal attire to an interview is common, it isn't always the right choice. You can also try talking to a current or former employee of the place you are interviewing or drive to the company's location around 4:30 P.M. and see how employees are dressed when they are leaving the office. Your goal is to dress appropriately for the environment you want to join. You want to STAND OUT! but not stick out like a sore thumb.

In the last chapter, I'll share about how to deal with the end of a job interview. First impressions are powerful, but last impressions are equally important.

13

Closing Strong

SOMETIMES THE END of a job interview winds down naturally, and other times there's an abrupt hard stop. Either way, you should be prepared to end the interview in the driver's seat. Job candidates who have an endgame in mind STAND OUT! over those who don't. In this chapter, we'll review what to say before you shake hands and walk out of the room. My methodology might be a bit uncomfortable if you've never had any sales training, but with a little practice, you'll ace the end of the interview.

Remember I'm a professional sales trainer. I use my sales training to help job candidates get offers. You've heard the phrase "close the deal." In sales terms, closing is generally defined as the moment when the salesperson asks the prospect for their business. It's when a contract is signed and a financial transaction takes place. And if a salesperson doesn't close the deal, there is no deal. It doesn't matter how much the prospect was "wowed" during the sales presentation. It might sound a bit simplistic, but the reality is that the diminishing production of a salesperson starts with the inability to close the sale. Good closers are good salespeople.

> Near the end of the job interview, you need to be a good closer.

Near the end of the job interview, you need to be a good closer. Obviously, you're not going to get an offer right then and there (although it DOES happen), but you can go a long way toward getting an offer if you use the same closing techniques good salespeople use. Let me explain.

At the end of a sales presentation, as in an interview, a good closer revisits and summarizes. You want to remind the prospective buyer, which in this case is the hiring manager, why you are such a great candidate for the position. You can be frank and matter-of-fact about this; it doesn't need to come across as boasting. Just be honest in your assessment and describe why you think you are so well-suited for the job. Remember the interviewer is talking to a lot of people and taking a lot of notes. What you say about yourself at the end of the interview is going to end up in those notes. You can simplify this for the interviewer with your summary.

First, summarize what you've learned about the job. Describe it in some detail and ask if you're describing the role correctly. Then simply explain, based on your background and experience, why you're so well-suited for this role. You can review what's already been said during the interview, but of course more briefly. Some interviewers might be surprised by how you take control of the interview in this way, to your advantage. You will STAND OUT, because very few candidates will do this during an interview. It gives you a unique edge.

Then—and this might be a little uncomfortable for you—I highly recommend that you ask if the hiring manager has any reservations about you. You can simply say, "Based on our discussions today, do you have any reservations about me as a candidate for this role?" This really puts the interviewer on the spot, right? It also puts you on the spot. But you want to clear everything up during the interview. It does not help you to leave an interview if the hiring manager has unanswered questions about you. In fact, if there are unanswered questions, you're probably not getting an offer. Encourage the interviewer in a tactful way to reveal his concerns right then and there. And if the interviewer offers any constructive criticism, agree with the perceived concern or ask for further clarification, but also offer your counter. Explain why you believe you can overcome those objections and also confirm how you would prioritize the concerns relative to your other skills. Do it with a smile.

> I highly recommend that you ask if the hiring manager has any reservations about you.

Closing Strong

This closing strategy is an important part of my STAND OUT! methodology. The job candidates I mentor tell me it works. If anything, you will leave the interview not only in a stronger position, but you'll probably also leave knowing if you're in the running.

One of the last suggestions that I will make to STAND OUT is to let the interviewer know that you will follow up and provide a 30-60-90 day onboarding plan that will reflect your ideas and suggestions on how best to optimize your success in the role. I promise you that this approach will put you on another level with the interviewer and demonstrate that you are organized and an excellent communicator. *(See downloadable 30-60-90 template on website (www.orderstandout.com).*

14

Mastering Video Interviews

DO YOU HAVE a video interview on your schedule? As more employees are working remotely, video interviews have become commonplace. For hiring managers, video interviews get the process started faster than scheduling them in person. For some positions, the entire process may be handled virtually, while others may have a combination of video and in-person interviews. Video interviewing is an entirely different scenario, and it's important that you prepare for it differently than for an in-person interview.

> For hiring managers, video interviews get the process started faster than scheduling them in person.

What I'll share here seems like common, ordinary advice. But you'd be surprised at how many people fail at video interviews. Follow these tips, and you will STAND OUT, even on video.

First, do a trial run. Check your webcam and any headset or microphone as if you were going to do the actual interview. If possible, use the same video technology that you'll be using during the actual interview. That way, you won't have any last-minute installation issues or password problems right before your interview. This will lessen your anxiety going into it.

In terms of your camera, the angle is quite important. A poorly placed camera can result in an unflattering double chin or weird shadows. Place your webcam level with your eyes or slightly higher. Often a webcam is situated too low, and people don't look their best in a camera angle that's coming from beneath their chin. Grab a couple of books and place them under your laptop if necessary. Get that webcam up above your eyes, but not so much that the hiring manager is looking down on you.

Along with webcam height, one of the problems of the too-low webcam is that the background becomes a giant white ceiling, which doesn't look that great. A right-height webcam allows for a more pleasing background. What's in your specific background doesn't matter all that much, so long as it's not distracting. You want your viewer to focus on *you*, not the pile of laundry on your bed. If you're using a laptop, you have a lot of flexibility to take it wherever you can get the background you want.

You want the interviewer to see your head and shoulders, and not much below your shoulders. You might get in a little tighter than you normally would for a video call. Again, experiment.

Make sure to use plenty of light, and also that you're not backlit—the light should come from in front of you (behind your webcam) or from the side, but not from behind. You may want to try putting a lamp on or near your desk so that it lights up your face. Try different ways of lighting yourself, avoiding glare and washout, creating a pleasing and clear image.

> Turn off your phone and any alerts on your computer to avoid getting thrown off by emails or instant messages during the interview.

This also goes without saying, but I'll say it because it becomes a problem with way too many interviews. Try to mitigate all other background noise, including noise from pets and people. Also turn off your phone and any alerts on your computer to avoid getting thrown off by emails or instant messages during the interview. The microphone will pick up any noise in the room, so don't tap your pen or shuffle papers.

Finally, make eye contact and maintain good posture. Look at the black dot! It can feel awkward because you're literally looking at a little black dot instead of the person you're conversing with, but just relax with it, smile, and pretend the black dot is the person. Otherwise, you'll get distracted by looking at yourself when you're talking. Avoid looking at yourself altogether.

It's easy to STAND OUT! when you do job interviews by video, because so few people do them correctly. Follow these tips, and you'll go directly to the top of the pile!

15

The Post-Interview Follow-up

YOU MIGHT THINK that your job interview is over once you walk out of the office or click out of the video platform. But you'd be wrong. The evaluation process continues even after the interview has concluded. Place yourself in the shoes of the job interviewer. After interviewing dozens (or more) candidates, the decision is probably not very clear. In fact it's sometimes hard to even remember each candidate and place a name with a face. So once you have completed the interview process, there are a few things you can do to STAND OUT and be remembered.

> The evaluation process continues even after the interview has concluded. Place yourself in the shoes of the job interviewer.

This can be a little confusing, especially if you are working with a recruiter. But it's worth clarifying that your follow-up is a crucial part of the decision-making process, even if you're being represented by a recruiter. Remember a recruiter has many clients and although they have your best interests in mind, it's always best to make sure that you've got your own best interests in mind as well.

> You'd be surprised how much weight other staff have on the interview process, particularly those people who are close to the interviewer.

So how do you follow-up in such a way that you truly STAND OUT, and who do you follow-up with?

First, you want to send a "Thank You" email to everyone you interacted with during the process, from the receptionist to the most senior person you engaged with along the way. They all matter when it comes to creating the best impression possible. In fact, some organizations include the receptionist in the decision-making process by asking them to engage you in conversation while you wait. You'd be surprised how much weight other staff have on the interview process, particularly those people who are close to the interviewer.

How soon should you follow-up?

As soon as possible. Don't wait. It demonstrates a sense of urgency on your part. It won't make you seem desperate so don't worry about creating that impression. The company you are interviewing with is more desperate than you are in almost every case. They need to hire someone soon, so never be bashful or timid about reaching out post-interview.

So what should I say?

You should start by thanking them for their time or assistance during the interview process.

Secondly, you should recognize them for any achievements, honors, or notable events (a wedding, birth of baby, etc.) that you learned about during your conversation. Next, you should repeat back what you learned from them during the interview. This demonstrates that you are a good listener and an effective communicator. Lastly, let them know what excites you about the opportunity and why you feel like you are a good fit.

What should I do if I feel like it's not the right fit for me?

You should repeat all of the same steps as above, with the exception of the last step. Instead, you let them know that you don't feel like it is not the type of role that you are considering at this time and why. Then let them know what type of role you would be interested in something like that became available. This alone may cause them to reconsider how they think about the roles within their organization and make a change. You may wonder why even communicate this if you don't want the job. Never burn a bridge! There may be similar jobs within the organization that are a good fit, or

> Effective follow-up is the single most common step that candidates neglect to do.

they may even want to change the position to make it a better fit for you.

Effective follow-up is the single most common step that candidates neglect to do, so applying a little extra effort can make all of the difference. Less than 10% of job candidates today do any sort of post-interview follow-up. I guarantee you'll STAND OUT if you do!

16

The Offer

CONGRATULATIONS, YOU HAVE an offer! Now what?

When you receive an offer of employment, it can be very exciting but sometimes disappointing assuming your expectations were not met. Try to remain objective about things and look at the bigger picture, if possible. You should be proud that you made it through the interview process, and hopefully this book made a positive difference in the outcome.

Remember that once you receive a job offer, you probably have more leverage right there and then to address your job description and to improve compensation than you will down the line. This is your time to step back and think expansively about your new work and your quality of life. Take some time and make sure the position is in alignment with your goals and your compensation is workable. Then negotiate, if neccesary.

Here's what's important to remember after you receive an offer. Other than compensation, there are *many* other factors that are worth evaluating as part of the overall package.

> Other than compensation, there are *many* other factors that are worth evaluating as part of the overall package.

Here are some of those considerations. Ask yourself the following questions:

How much will I learn in this role over the next few years?

The ability to advance in your career will directly correlate to how much you learn in your career. So if you are simply changing companies to perform the same function somewhere else, then you may have to work independently to develop the knowledge necessary to take you to the next level. This is all about long term career growth so try not to focus exclusively on the short-term.

Is there a variable component of my compensation and how likely is that I will achieve the goals necessary to realistically receive the income?

Variable compensation components include bonuses, commission, profit sharing, or other non-salaried financial benefits. These components are often based on positive outcomes, not status quo and certainly not negative, so just make sure that you understand how realistic the targets are based on last year's accomplishments. If they don't appear realistic, then you could always counter with somewhat lower targets. Don't assume the best, nor the worst.

Is working remotely an option?

Be careful with this benefit. While it can provide some flexibility to your day-to-day, it can also prohibit you from getting the kind of exposure you may want to advance within the company. Being in the office with other senior leadership can make it much easier for you to participate in important ad-hoc discussions and decisions being made. So be careful how you value this benefit depending on your career goals and objectives.

Is the company growing? Or struggling to grow?

This factor alone could drive much of your decision when you evaluate the overall offer. A growing company will present more opportunities for you to be promoted than one that is not growing, generally speaking. That's not to say that there aren't opportunities to be promoted at companies that are not growing. It's just not as likely. A lower than expected offer from a strong, growing company is going to be a better opportunity than a higher than expected offer from a struggling and weaker company. You'll simply have more opportunities to grow in your career with a better company, so keep this in mind.

There are several other considerations as well, but evaluating these additional aspects of the offer can help you make a decision between more than one offer assuming you are lucky enough to have multiple offers. Depending on the types of compensation included in the offer, you may want to have an attorney review the terms and conditions so that you have a clear understanding of what is being offered and to fully understand what conditions. Particularly, when stock options or equity is

> Have an attorney review the terms and conditions so that you have a clear understanding of what is being offered and to fully understand what conditions.

involved because there are several different types and the tax obligations can be very different.

Don't forget to acknowledge the offer immediately. Don't delay, and be gracious. Communicate clearly that you need a little time to review the offer, but don't wait more than a few days. Then after you accept or counter-offer, remember that you can't negotiate everything — and that once you've agreed on something, you can't go back on it. If you counter-offer, be well-prepared, respectful and constructive. You sold yourself, so be confident in your counter-offer, but at the same time don't be greedy.

For more information about the Stand Out series and other Stand Out events, please visit www.orderstandout.com.

CPSIA information can be obtained
at www.ICGtesting.com
Printed in the USA
BVHW070915060123
655718BV00008B/689